A Readers' Guide to
Reza Aslan's
Zealot

By Patrick J. Goggins

Independently published in Hollywood, Florida

© Patrick J. Goggins, 2013, 2018

ISBN: 9781983007651

Contents

Preface

Two stories emerge when discussing Reza Aslan's Zealot: The Life and Times of Jesus of Nazareth (Aslan, 2013): one is scriptural, the other is cultural. Zealot's story is a cautionary tale about diving head first into the culture wars and emerging unscathed.

The cultural story outlined in Chapter I of this review looks at how an everyday attack on Contrary Information by an agenda-driven news outlet created such a backlash, it had the unintended consequence of catapulting the Contrary Information front and center into the national discussion. Chapter II provides an extremely condensed look at Aslan's views on Jesus of Nazareth, the historical Jesus. Chapter III outlines Aslan's perspective on the early Christian church; how Jesus of Nazareth became Jesus Christ. Chapter IV explores what religious scholars and the commentariat are saying about Zealot. Chapter V attempts to make some sense of it all.

SPOILER ALERT! This guide discusses many of Aslan's observations and conclusions. If you are reading or intend to read *Zealot* (which I highly recommend), do yourself a favor, close this window, and purchase the book here.

Also, a preface may be in order. This territory has been covered repeatedly for centuries by very smart people who have spent many collective lifetimes studying it. One thing that can be said definitively is that the historical record has gone cold. There is virtually no new material, and few new interpretations of it. In the twenty years Aslan spent studying this material, living with it even, it is likely that he only encountered a small fraction of it. This guide is built on only a small fraction of the fraction that Aslan studied so, by definition, it is the work of an amateur.

It should also go without saying that every one of Aslan's conclusions are disputed, even the ones that would seem uncontroversial. According to Aslan, most of his observations are supported by the greater weight of academic thought. For the most part, this guide takes him at his word, and consequently does not reference competing views. Refer to the notes at the end of *Zealot* for a discussion of some competing views. This guide also does not continuously cite to Aslan, otherwise every paragraph would begin "According to Aslan." Where quotes appear, they are from *Zealot*, unless otherwise attributed.

Of course, *Zealot* touches on a subject that many people find very emotionally charged. This guide is didactic which, is counter-intuitive, because it is written by an amateur. So it fails its purpose. Take it then for what it is, a journey down a very familiar path, with an eye out for new discoveries.

Chapter I: The Green Controversy

Never before has a writer owed so much to a bad interview. Lauren Green's July 26, 2013 FoxNews.com interview made Reza Aslan a national celebrity, and made his book a *cause célèbre*. *Zealot* was released on July 16th. The publisher anticipated that the book would have broad appeal, so they arranged for Aslan to promote it in the media. The firestorm started with a July 24th column on FoxNews.com by John S. Dickerson, who wrote: "Media reports have introduced Aslan as a 'religion scholar' but have failed to mention that he is a devout Muslim." (Dickerson, 2013).

Whatever a "religion scholar" is, Dickerson is not one. He is an evangelical minister and motivational speaker who has published a book and a few op-ed pieces on evangelism. He did not have the academic credentials to criticize *Zealot*, but he did have a hook on *Zealot* that resonated with FoxNews' producers: ignore the content, attack the author!

Pastor Dickerson packs his unconvincing "objectivity" argument with so many logical fallacies that it would take an undergraduate philosophy major a month to tease them all out: "[Aslan] is not an objective observer, but, to use his own word, a zealot, with religious motivation to destroy what Western culture has believed about its central figure for hundreds of years." Was Aslan religiously motivated to destroy Western beliefs of Jesus Christ? First, that is like saying that racial prejudice motivated George Zimmerman to stop Trayvon Martin. It is impossible to determine what motivates someone else. More importantly, had Pastor Dickerson actually read the book, he would have seen (with some exceptions outlined below) that *Zealot* is merely a survey and interpretation of generally accepted current biblical scholarship.

Lauren Green's FoxNews producers stepped up the fabricated controversy a notch by quoting Pastor Dickerson in what is now probably the world's most watched interview of a biblical scholar – ever. (Green, 2013) There is certainly no need to re-hash Green's bungled interview here except to emphasize that: first, she clearly had not read *Zealot*, or even a synopsis of it, second, she tenaciously stuck to her single talking point, *i.e.* that the author failed to disclose that he is a Muslim, and third, her interview probably pushed his book to the top of the bestseller list.

FoxNews' conclusion that *Zealot* is driven by an Islamic anti-Christian agenda goes against what is actually written in the book. For instance, Islam teaches that Jesus was not killed by crucifixion or any other means. Aslan contradicts that teaching by emphasizing the historicity of the crucifixion. FoxNews' uninformed criticism is irresponsible and dangerous, promoting Islamophobia instead of informed dialogue.

One biblical scholar dismisses the claim that Aslan's religion precludes him from writing the book: "Aslan clearly respects and admires Jesus. That some Christians might find his claims unsettling is, well, tough, because Aslan is doing serious intellectual work. The complaints have no

place in responsible public discourse."
(Carey, 2013)

That is not to say that Aslan came out of
the Green interview completely unscathed
– he did misrepresent his credentials not
once, but twice. When questioned, Aslan
said repeatedly, "I am a historian, I am a
Ph.D in the history of religions." This is in
fact not true. (Hallowell, 2013). Aslan has
a Ph.D in the *sociology* of religions from
the University of California, Santa
Barbara. He also has a bachelor's of
religious studies from Santa Clara
University, a master's of theological
studies from Harvard Divinity School, and
a master's of fine arts in creative writing
from the University of Iowa – but not a
Ph.D in the history of religions, as he
claimed. The fact that his degree is in the
sociology of religion and not the *history*
of religion probably does not make a
difference in terms of his qualifications to
write the book, but it also does not change
the fact that he claimed to have
credentials that he did not have. That is a
big no-no in academic circles, one that
should not lightly be dismissed as a slip of
the tongue.

That said, the Green interview seemed more like a Punch and Judy puppet show than a high-minded clash between religious fundamentalism and academic freedom. Green and Aslan both were clearly prepared for what would transpire in the ten minute interview, they merely acted out the respective roles that were thrust upon them. Both repeated their points over and over. To sum up the entire interview:

> Green: You didn't disclose that you're a Muslim, and as a Muslim, how can you write objectively about Jesus?

> Aslan: I did disclose that I am a Muslim, and I can write objectively about Jesus because I am a fully qualified scholar.

While Aslan clearly won this battle, neither Aslan nor Green even made a pretense of having an actual discourse – that wasn't the point. Both were only puffing to their respective audiences. That's the paradigm for succeeding in the age of New Media: speak to your base and let confirmation bias weed out your opponent's rebuttals.

Reaction to the Green interview was loud and immediate. The interview, which only aired on FoxNews' website, went viral. On July 27th, Buzzfeed posted the video under the banner, "Is This the Most Embarrassing Interview Fox News Has Ever Done?" The overwhelming reaction was to condemn Green and FoxNews for assuming that a Muslim scholar could not be objective about Christianity. It was an interesting dynamic to observe. Just as the Middle East has been defining the borders between religious fundamentalism and mainstream thought since the fall of Saddam and the Arab Spring, so has the United States been struggling with its own conversation between Christianity and Islam. There are fundamentalists in both the U.S. and the Middle East who seem to want nothing less than a holy war. Hopefully, the more rational voices will prevail, but today that is far from certain. All it takes is one car bomb to inflame popular passions.

The conservative reaction to *Zealot* was, again, to attack the author. Once the attack went viral, perhaps given the strength of their position, liberal and mainstream voices came together in mutual condemnation of FoxNews' take on the book. Not wanting to miss the party, Glen Beck weighed in on July 31st, sporting chin whiskers and accusing Aslan of the unforgivable: "Who is he? He is a radical progressive." For its part, FoxNews has been in full retreat since. FoxNews has not published a word on *Zealot* since running an August 2nd op-ed entitled "Liberal media sharks continue feeding frenzy over 'Zealot' interview." (Gainor, 2013). It appears that even then, there was still some meat left on that bone.

The Green interview generated a buzz that correlated directly into sales. After the video was viewed on Buzzfeed over 5.3 million times, Random House printed an additional 180,000 copies of *Zealot*. As of August 11th, *Zealot* was the New York Times' number one on the combined print and e-book non-fiction list. It remained number one for three weeks.

So the net result of the Green controversy was to propel a book that debunks most commonly held Christian notions about the historical Jesus into water cooler and dinner table conversations across the country. That is probably not quite what FoxNews was trying to accomplish, but that's how New Media works. You live by the buzz, you die by the buzz.

The question remains, what is it in *Zealot* that was so controversial to FoxNews' producers?

Chapter II: The Story of Jesus of Nazareth

Aslan devotes roughly equal portions of *Zealot* to the historical Jesus of Nazareth, and to the political and cultural context of first century Palestine. This is one of the book's strongest points – understanding the cultural and political context is particularly helpful in understanding the man who would later become Christ.

Zealot is written for the general reader (about an 8th grade reading level), and it is grouped by topic, yet Aslan assumes the reader knows the chronology of the Roman occupation of Palestine. For instance, while in life, Jesus met John the Baptist before entering into Jerusalem, in *Zealot*, Aslan discusses Jesus' entry into Jerusalem in Chapter 6, before the discussion of John the Baptist in Chapter 7. This forces readers to keep going back to a mental timeline, skipping back and forth, making it difficult to follow. Aslan does provide a cursory timeline mid-way through the book, but a more thorough chronological history of Roman occupation and the Judean resistance in the beginning of the text would have been helpful. So, in case your knowledge of first century Judean history is a little thin, here is the chronology missing from *Zealot*:

The First Temple was built in Jerusalem by Solomon and sacked and destroyed by the Babylonian Nebuchadnezzar II in 586 B.C.E. The Second Temple was built by Zerubbabel in 516 B.C.E. and later re-built from the foundation up by Herod the Great. The Temple was of vital importance to Second Temple Judaism. In addition to being the seat of government, the center of commerce, and the central bank, the Second Temple was the physical center of the faith. The sacrifices made there were mandated by the laws of the God of Abraham and were scrupulously observed by the faithful.

Rome's occupation of Palestine began in 63 B.C.E., when Roman General Pompey defeated Syria in the Third Mithridatic War. In order to control popular uprisings, Rome divided Palestine into administrative districts. (Schiffman, n.d.). Each district was ruled by a Jewish tetrarch and a Roman governor. The tetrarchs were to Rome what "client states" are to the U.S. – friendly governments installed by an occupying force.

Like every empire before and since, the Roman Empire's principal objective was the acquisition of wealth. Judea's sole purpose in the Roman Empire was to pay taxes. The Romans assured that the Judeans paid their taxes by vesting the priestly class, a "handful of wealthy priestly families who maintained the Temple cult," with the right to collect taxes, and of course to keep a portion for themselves. The Romans consolidated power by appointing the High Priest, thus controlling the Temple.

The Romans rarely banned the local religious cults in the lands they occupied. More often, over time, rival gods were assimilated into the pagan Roman cult. For instance, worship of Ba'al was Romanized over time to worship of Saturn. (Wilson, 2003).

Again and again, Aslan emphasizes that there was a particularly strong messianic movement in first century Palestine. The

Jews fervently awaited a messiah "who would return the Jews to their previous position of power and glory," that is, the days of the First Temple when the twelve tribes of the Israelites were united. There were many self-proclaimed messiahs in Judea at the time, such as Theudas, Athronges, Hezekiah, Simon of Peraea, Judas the Galilean, Menahem, Simon son of Giora, Simon son of Kochba, as well ones known cryptically as "the Egyptian" and "the Samaritan." Some of these would-be messiahs led armed revolts against the Romans. Many of them were charged with sedition by the Romans and executed.

The term *messiah* means "anointed one" which, in the context of Second Temple Judaism, meant a descendant of King David, who was God's representative on earth. The messiah's purpose was to re-establish the land of Israel. By definition, that meant ridding Palestine of Rome. According to Aslan, "to call oneself the messiah [in first-century Palestine] was tantamount to declaring war on Rome."

Jesus' story took place in the district known as Judea. In 37 B.C.E., Rome installed Herod the Great as their client king in Judea. His reign was marked by massive construction projects and savage executions of dissenters. Among his ambitious projects was rebuilding the Second Temple, from the foundation up. He irked many devout Jews, though, by including tributes to the Roman gods in the Second Temple. It was blasphemy, but Herod the Great controlled the priesthood, so dissent was muted.

The year 27 B.C.E. marked the end of the Roman Republic and the beginning of the Roman Empire – Augustus Caesar succeeded Claudius to become the first Roman Emperor. In 4 B.C.E., Herod the Great died and Judea was divided in three provinces. Galilee went to his son Herod Antipas. In 6 C.E., Rome assumed direct control of Jerusalem.

Sometime between the death of Herod the Great in 4 B.C.E, and Rome's assumption of direct control over Jerusalem in 6 C.E., a boy name Yeshu was born to a woman named Miryām. Yeshu's name would later be Romanized to Jesus, Miryām to Mary. That much is commonly accepted as true, or as academics put it, its "historicity" is not in doubt. The "historicity" of nearly everything else about Jesus' birth has at least been debated.

One debate centers around Jesus's patrimony. In the Gospel of Mark, Jesus is referred to as "the son of Mary." Given that names then were patrilineal, this is strange, leading to speculation that Jesus may have been illegitimate. One theory, based on the writings of Origen, was that Mary may have been raped (or at least impregnated) by a Roman soldier named Pantera. According to the bible, when Mary was found to be pregnant, she had not lived with Joseph, to whom she was engaged, and he did not have relations with her before the child was born. (Matthew 1:18-25) There is very little historic dispute that Jesus had many siblings. The gospels name several, including James, Joseph, Simon, and Judas.

Jesus was likely born in Nazareth, not Bethlehem. Addressing the trip to

Bethlehem, Aslan points out that historically, there never was a Roman census in Galilee. Even if there was such a census, practically speaking, no one would have been required to travel to a distant land just to be counted, especially since their taxable property (which after all is what the Romans really wanted to count) would be where people actually lived, not in their home towns. Aslan adds that the Bethlehem birth narrative is contradicted by Jesus' own words in the gospels. When a Pharisee points out that the messiah could not come from Galilee, Jesus admits the point, saying "You know me, and you know where I am from." John 7:28.

Aslan describes the virgin birth as a "contentious creation." Both the oldest canonical gospel (Mark,) and the most recent canonical gospel (John,) completely omit any mention of the virgin birth. Likewise, there is no mention of the virgin birth in the Pauline epistles, the oldest books in the bible. Only Luke and Matthew pursue the account of the virgin birth. The Gospel of Matthew in particular devotes a significant amount of attention to the infancy narrative. Aslan points out that the virgin birth was possibly inserted in Luke and Matthew to convince Jewish readers that the prophesy in Isaiah 7:14 was fulfilled in Jesus: "Therefore, the Lord, of His own, shall give you a sign; behold, the (*alma*) is with child, and she shall bear a son, and she shall call his name Immanuel." As Aslan notes, if this is so, Luke and Matthew may have been operating off of a mis-reading of Isaiah, as the word *alma* unequivocally refers to a young woman, not a virgin.

Perhaps recognizing the intensity of Marian devotion as compared to the biological limitations of the dogmas of virgin birth (that Jesus was conceived without a man) and perpetual virginity (that Mary was virgin even after birth and remained so throughout her life), Aslan's discussion of the virgin birth is rather thin. He does not discuss, for instance, the contradiction between immaculate conception doctrine, which says that God was Jesus's *father*, and the "seed of David" argument, which says that the messiah's *father* would be from Bethlehem, "the village where David was." (John 7:42). Clearly, the people promoting Jesus as David's seed were not claiming that he was conceived immaculately by God. Aslan also does not mention that the Qur'an holds that Jesus was born of a virgin (another instance where Aslan's views differ from Islam). Further, he does not discuss the feminist critique of Mariology (which includes the dogma of perpetual virginity) as being the result of a patriarchal mindset intended to limit the role of women in the church.

In 14 C.E., Augustus Caesar died and was succeeded by Tiberius Caesar. In 26 C.E., Rome sent Pontius Pilate to Jerusalem as the city's fifth prefect. Pilate appointed Joseph Caiaphas as the high priest.

As a youth, Jesus was likely illiterate, spoke Aramaic, and worked in the construction trade. Aslan goes to some length conjecturing that Jesus may have worked in the growing city of Sepphoris and was introduced there to anti-Roman nationalist zealots, but acknowledges there is no historical proof (or refutation) of this assertion. Aslan also points out that there is no evidence one way or another whether Jesus was married, although "it would have been almost unthinkable for a thirty-year-old Jewish male in Jesus's time not to have a wife."

Somewhere around this time Jesus got caught up in the messianic fervor of first century Judea. As Aslan puts it, "In 28 C.E., an ascetic preacher named John began baptizing people in the waters of the Jordan River, initiating them into what he believed was the true nation of Israel." Jesus would become a follower of John the Baptist, who Aslan posits may have been an Essene, part of a messianic cult that preached "Prepare the way of the Lord, make straight the paths of our God." Isaiah 40:3.

Aslan reviews the gospel accounts of the interactions between John the Baptist and Jesus, and concludes that they were designed to show that Jesus was somehow "superior" to John, when the historical record is rather clear that Jesus was baptized by John, and that Jesus "very likely began his ministry as just another of [John the Baptist's] disciples." He notes that Jesus's first disciples, Andrew and Philip, were former followers of John the Baptist.

Two years later, Herod Antipas had John the Baptist arrested and put to death, either for his growing popularity or for his criticism of Antipas' illegal marriage to his brother's wife. The story that John the Baptist was killed at the request of the toothsome Salome, who wanted his head on a plate, is probably just (moderately sexy) literature. Regardless, after John the Baptist's death, Jesus took up his ministry, traveling through Galilee (north of Jerusalem), avoiding the larger cities, preaching from town to town.

Jesus gathered disciples along the way. Ultimately, Jesus collected seventy-two disciples more or less, among them many women, all of whom followed him as he preached. Only a select few made up "the Twelve," chosen either by Jesus or the gospel writers to represent the twelve tribes of Israel.

The gospels recount how Jesus performed many miracles. Aslan points out that these were probably the biggest "draw" in his ministry. There is more historical proof supporting Jesus's miracles than his birth in Nazareth and his death at Golgotha, but Aslan puts them in context, pointing out Judea was a culture steeped in magic and exorcism: "Jesus's status as an exorcist and miracle worker may seem unusual, even absurd, to modern skeptics, but it did not deviate greatly from the standard expectation of exorcists and miracle workers in first-century Palestine" such as Eleazar, Rabbi Simon ben Yohai, Apollonius of Tyana, Rabbi Hanina ben Dosa, Abba Hilqiah and Hanan the Hidden, and Honi the Circle-Drawer.

Like Jesus, Theudas and "the Egyptian" also performed miracles and were would-be messiahs. Jesus's early detractors claimed that his miracles were really just magic. According to Aslan, "Magic and miracle are perhaps best thought of as two sides of the same coin in ancient Palestine." To this day, the Catholic church maintains a rite of exorcism and believes in angels. Aslan further emphasizes that Jesus's miracles challenged the priestly code and (perhaps stretching a bit) invalidated the very purpose of the Temple priesthood.

What we do know is that Jesus preached what might today be known as a preference for the poor. His social justice message was accessible to the people of Galilee because he preached in the Galilean's native Aramaic, not the Greek used by the scribes and priests. Typical is the story of the rich ruler, who asked Jesus what he needed to do to inherit eternal life. When the ruler explained that he had kept all of God's commandments, Jesus told him:

> "There is still one thing lacking. Sell all that you own and distribute the money to the poor, and you will have treasure in heaven; then come, follow me." But when [the ruler] heard this, he became sad; for he was very rich. Jesus looked at him and said, "How hard it is for those who have wealth to enter the kingdom of God! Indeed, it is easier for a camel to go through the eye of a needle than for someone who is rich to enter the kingdom of God." Luke 18:22-25.

In Chapter 10 of *Zealot*, Aslan emphasizes the nationalist aspect of Jesus' ministry: "Of this there can be no doubt: the central theme and unifying message of Jesus's brief three-year ministry was the promise of the Kingdom of God. Practically everything Jesus said or did in the gospels served the function of publicly proclaiming the Kingdom's coming." Given the social justice emphasis of Jesus's ministry, this is simply incorrect. Further, the meaning of the term "Kingdom of God" throughout the canonical gospels themselves is vague. Aslan says that Jesus's message was that the Kingdom of God was coming to earth.[1] But, as the above passage from Luke

---

[1] Not to get overly nit-picky, but Aslan discusses Jesus's statement to Pilate that "My kingdom is not of this world" recounted in John 18:36. Aslan says the phrase *ouk estin ek tou kosmou* "is perhaps better translated as 'not part of this order/system [of government].'" (p.117) This interpretation seems to be incorrect. First, Aslan pointedly omits the rest of the passage, in which Jesus says, "If my kingdom were from this world, my followers would be fighting to keep me from being handed over to the Jews. But as it is, my kingdom is not from here."Also, the word *kosmou* is used seventy-two times in the New Testament, each time referring to the first century cosmological conception of the planet earth, not to any system of government.

illustrates, some canonical passages indicate that Jesus's ministry was more about *getting in* to the Kingdom of God. Jesus's simple prescription to enter the Kingdom of God? Sell what you have and give the money to the poor.

As time passed and the crowds grew, Jesus's message became increasingly more critical of the priestly caste, appointed by Rome, whom Jesus deemed imposters occupying God's Temple. One interpretation of the Parable of the Good Samaritan (Luke 10:29-37) is that it was not in praise of the Samaritan who helped the unfortunate who had been robbed, beaten, and left for dead, but rather a criticism of the priests who refused to help him.

In about 30 C.E., Jesus and his followers entered into Jerusalem. The gospel accounts have Jesus riding a donkey, flanked by a cheering crowd. The entrance, or the account of the entrance, was in Aslan's view, "orchestrated" to fulfill the prophesy in Zechariah 9:9 ("Lo, your king comes to you; triumphant and victorious is he, humble and riding on a donkey.")

The next day, Jesus and his followers entered the Temple and set about "cleansing" it. In a rage, he overturned the tables of the money changers in the Court of the Gentiles and drove out the vendors hawking cheap food and souvenirs. The Romans investigating the ruckus found Jesus standing in the Temple courtyard, saying, "It is written: My house shall be called a house of prayer for all nations. But you have made it a den of thieves." Aslan does not address whether this might have been an anti-Roman gesture, as the only coins in the Temple were the Roman's.

Oddly, in the biblical account, Jesus was not arrested after the cleansing of the Temple. Instead, the priests asked Jesus to justify the vandalism. "Destroy this Temple," Jesus said enigmatically, "and in three days I will raise it up." The priests then asked Jesus if it was lawful (meaning under Mosaic Law) to pay tribute to Caesar. Aslan casts this question as a trap set by the priests to corner Jesus into admitting that he was a zealot who wanted to oust Rome, and therefore was guilty of sedition. Jesus replied "render to Caesar what belongs to Caesar, and render unto God that which belongs to God." A common interpretation of this reply is that Jesus was distinguishing between worldly and other-worldy possessions. Aslan emphasizes that it was the coin itself that belonged to Caesar, which should be rendered unto Caesar, and that it was the land of Palestine that was God's, and therefore rightly should be rendered unto Him. Showing real admiration for this clever interpretation of Jesus's reply, Aslan says, "That is the zealot argument in its simplest, most concise form."

Jesus had a Passover meal with his disciples that evening, and after, repaired to Gethsemane where a cohort of Roman guards and Temple police arrested him. Jesus was charged with "forbidding us to pay taxes to the emperor, and saying that he himself is the Messiah, a king," charges that Jesus did not deny. (Luke 23:2)

The biblical accounts of Jesus's crucifixion begin with the hearing before Caiaphas, where Jesus was questioned about his supposed promise to destroy the Temple and to raise it up in three days. Aslan points out that a nighttime hearing at the Sanhedrin during Passover would not have been permitted by Jewish law, and even then, the "trial" would have been quite brief and, if Jesus was convicted of blasphemy, he would have been stoned to death then and there, not handed over to the Roman authorities.

Still, gospel accounts have Jesus brought before Pontius Pilate for a second trial. Aslan posits that it is unlikely that a Jewish peasant would have gotten a trial in front of Pontius Pilate in the first place, but considering that Jerusalem was packed with Passover crowds, perhaps a trial was held to maintain public order (which implies that it would have been more theater than judicial proceeding – its result pre-determined).

If there was a trial, it would have been because Jesus was charged with sedition. Aslan argues that it is highly unlikely that Pilate would have deferred to the crowd's will as between Jesus and Barabbas:

"What is truly beyond belief is the portrayal of Pontius Pilate – a man renowned for his loathing of the Jews...spending even a moment of his time pondering the fate of yet another Jewish rabble-rouser." Other than context, he has no factual support for this argument. Aslan calls the accounts of the trial before Pilate "a patently fictitious scene," written for a Roman audience, to shift blame for Jesus's death from the Romans to the Jews. For the Jews to cry "we have no king but Caesar!" would be highly unlikely, even blasphemous, in an occupied land.

All accounts do agree that Jesus was crucified on Pontius Pilate's order. Jesus was scourged and crucified on Golgotha between two other men, whose *titulus* (the inscription hanging over their heads) read *lestai* or "bandits," a term used in Rome for insurrectionists, not simple thieves. Jesus's *titulus* read *Iēsus Nazarēnus, Rēx Iūdaeōrum* "Jesus the Nazarene, King of the Jews." Aslan emphasizes that this was not some mocking joke by the Roman authorities, but rather the actual description of the crime for which Jesus was being crucified – claiming to be a king. Under Roman law, claiming to be a king or a messiah meant sedition.

Aslan says, "Because the entire point of the crucifixion was to humiliate the victim and frighten the witnesses, the corpse would be left where it hung to be eaten by dogs and picked clean by birds of prey. The bones would be thrown onto a heap of trash, which is how Golgotha, the place of crucifixion, earned its name: the place of skulls... In a few short hours, Jesus's lungs would have tired, and breathing become impossible to sustain." At three o'clock on the day before the Sabbath, Jesus cried from the cross "My God, my God, why have you forsaken me?" He was given a sponge full of sour wine to relieve his suffering and then, with an agonized cry, Jesus of Nazareth breathed his last.

Whatever happened from that point did not happen to Jesus of Nazareth. That man was dead. What follows is the story of Jesus the Christ.

Chapter III: The Early Christian Church

Jesus's story did not end with his death. In some respects, that was only the beginning of the story. In about the year 30 C.E., on the fourteenth of Nisan, "the day of preparation" for the Passover, on a corpse-strewn hill near the gates of Jerusalem, the crucified body of an itinerant preacher was on display for all of the people entering and leaving the city to see. It was the body of Jesus of Nazareth. After the crucifixion, some of Jesus's disciples fled. Others gathered in Jerusalem where they waited, expecting his return as the messiah. They came to refer to their strict Mosaic Judaism, coupled with the belief that Jesus was the messiah, as "The Way."

After several years of waiting, there was a split between the members of The Way. One branch, the "mother assembly," was led by Jesus's brother James the Just. The mother assembly stayed in Jerusalem awaiting Jesus's return. The other branch, the Hellenized Jews of the Diaspora, led by the former Pharisee Paul, actively sought out Gentile converts and eventually split from Judaism to form a new religion – Christianity.

Perhaps James' message was inconvenient for a growing church that was actively seeking to grow. Paul's message was more appealing to those who wanted to enlarge The Way by converting Gentiles. Doctrinally, the focus came down to baptism of the uncircumcised, prohibited under Mosaic Law, but nonetheless advocated by the Pauline branch of The Way. Paul would ultimately prevail in this discussion, and thousands of Gentiles became baptized as Christians – a new religion unmoored from its Jewish roots. Aslan argues that the split between Christianity and Judaism came because it made the religion more palpable to the Romans, under whose rule the religion was practiced, and to the Gentiles, uncircumcised Greek speakers who were open to conversion from their various pagan cults. In short, greater doctrinal flexibility led to greater numbers which led, presumably, to more tithes.

Aslan recounts Stephen, who never met Jesus, but soon after the crucifixion encountered his disciples, "Galilean farmers and fishermen wandering about the Court of Gentiles, preaching about the simple Nazarean whom they called the messiah." Preachers, sectarians, and schismatics of all stripes would have been in Jerusalem at that time, seeking among the throngs of visiting Jews the broadest audience for their message. Jews from around the region would come to Jerusalem to worship and, for lack of a better word, vacation. The members of The Way, like most of the residents of Jerusalem, were poor, illiterate, and spoke Aramaic. The priests of the Temple were wealthy and spoke and read Hebrew and Greek. The diaspora Jews who could afford to travel to Jerusalem were also typically wealthier and better educated. Most of the Diaspora were Hellenized, meaning they spoke and wrote in Greek. Some were even Roman citizens.

Stephen was one such Hellenized diaspora Jew. What might have impressed him, Aslan speculates, is that one of these Galileans, a fisherman from Capernaum called Simon Peter, also known as Peter, claimed that Jesus's body was not left on the cross after the crucifixion. Instead, Jesus was taken down, buried in a tomb meant for a rich man, and three days later, rose from the dead. Simon Peter claimed to have seen the risen Jesus with his own eyes.

Aslan says that the historicity of the resurrection is "beyond the scope of any examination of the historical Jesus," which to some may seem like a cop-out. He does, though, point out the "nagging fact [that] one after another of those who claimed to have witnessed the risen Jesus went to their own gruesome deaths refusing to recant their testimony... They were being asked to deny something they themselves personally, directly encountered." He goes on, "Nevertheless, the fact remains that the resurrection is not a historical event...the event itself falls outside the scope of history and into the realm of faith." He adds, "Without the resurrection, the whole edifice of Jesus's claim to the mantle of the messiah comes crashing down."

Stephen was so impressed by these Galilean farmers, led by Jesus's own brother James, that Stephen abandoned his hometown, sold his possessions, and became a deacon in the nascent movement known as "The Way." The members of The Way considered themselves Jews, and strictly adhered to Mosaic Law, but believed that the resurrection proved that Jesus was the messiah. They lived communally in Jerusalem, preaching his word and awaiting his return. So taken was Stephen by the message of the risen Jesus, Stephen made an impassioned speech to the Sanhedrin, and for it, was stoned to death.

Stephen was the first martyr killed for preaching the word of Jesus. One witness to Stephen's death was a Pharisee named Saul of Tarsus. Saul was known as a vicious purger of blasphemies like the ones touted by Stephen. Like Stephen, many of Jesus's seventy-two disciples would also be brought before the Sanhedrin and stoned to death for blasphemy on the judgment of Pharisees such as Saul.

While they likely preached Jesus's word, such as the Lord's Prayer and the

Beatitudes, the resurrection story was a doctrinal problem for Jesus's disciples. Aslan points out that the concept of physical resurrection of the dead did not exist in Second Temple Judaism. For the Jews, the messiah would be someone who triumphed *and lived*. This story was completely new. Aslan also points out that the resurrection stories say that Jesus rose *according to the scriptures* (Luke 24:44-46: "Thus it is written that the messiah would suffer and rise again on the third day.") The problem, according to Aslan, is that "In the entire history of Jewish thought there is not a single line of scripture that says the messiah is to suffer, die, and rise again on the third day." This mis-statement of scripture likely brought with it a charge of blasphemy. The Pharisees no doubt cited their law to show that Jesus was actually accursed. ("Anyone hung on a tree is under God's curse." Deuteronomy 21:23)

As a result, without their charismatic preacher, Jesus's disciples' message was a tough sell among the scripture-literate Jews in Jerusalem.

Not so among the Hellenized diaspora Jews in cities such as Philippi, Corinth, Antioch, Alexandria, and Rome. As Greek speakers (and thinkers), the Hellenized Jews "were more receptive to the innovative interpretation of the scriptures being offered by Jesus's followers. In fact, it did not take long for these Greek-speaking Jews to outnumber the original Aramaic-speaking followers of Jesus in Jerusalem."

Soon enough, the Temple priests tired of Jesus's increasingly fervent Hellenist Jewish followers, and expelled them. These Hellenists left for Gentile cities such as Antioch, Ashdod, and Caesarea. "Little by little over the following decade, the Jewish sect founded by a group of rural Galileans morphed into a religion of urbanized Greek speakers. No longer bound by the confines of the Temple and the Jewish cult, the Hellenist preachers began to gradually shed Jesus's message of its nationalistic concerns, transforming it into a universal calling that would be more appealing to those living in a Greco-Roman milieu." Aslan adds, "Still, at this point, the Hellenists reserved their

preaching solely for their fellow Jews."
That would not last long.

In about 35 C.E., the apostle Peter
baptized a centurion named Cornelius, the
first Gentile to be baptized into The Way.
(Acts 10) Aslan calls the historicity of this
baptism "doubtful."

For several years after Jesus's death, Saul
of Tarsus continued his role among the
scribes prosecuting blasphemers at the
Sanhedrin. As the biblical account goes,
around 37 C.E., about seven years after
the crucifixion, Saul was walking down a
road, holding warrants for the arrest of
Jesus's followers in Damascus, when a
flashing light blinded him and Jesus's
voice called to him asking, "Saul, Saul,
why are you persecuting me?" Three days
later, a follower of Jesus laid hands on
Saul, who was then baptized into The
Way. Immediately, he began to preach
about Jesus. Saul claimed to have had
conversations with the risen Jesus, and
bore secret instructions intended solely
for his ears. He changed his name to Paul.

In his ministry, Paul traveled to Cyprus, Pisidian Antioch, Iconium, Lystra and Derbe claiming to have seen the risen Jesus with his own eyes, endowing himself with the same apostolic authority as the Twelve. Aslan does not discuss the so-called "incident at Antioch" where Paul publicly challenged Peter for compelling Gentile converts to The Way to "judaize," or adhere to Mosaic Laws such as circumcision, Sabbath observance, or observance of the Passover. Paul believed those laws were superseded by the "New Covenant" of Jesus Christ.

Paul would write "Am I not an apostle?... Have I not seen Jesus our Lord?" (1 Corinthians 9:1) There was a reason for the defensive tone of Paul's message. The "mother assembly" in Jerusalem sought to bring Jews into The Way by showing how Jesus's good news conformed with Mosaic Law. Paul had a different agenda. He sought converts among the Gentiles (non-Jews), and in order to accommodate their Greco-Roman culture and beliefs, Paul had become increasingly loose with the tenants of Mosaic Law, which he called a "ministry of death, chiseled in letters on

stone tablets." (2 Corinthians 3:7)
According to Aslan:

> "[It] was Paul who solved the disciples'
> dilemma of reconciling Jesus's shameful
> death on the cross with the messianic
> expectations of the Jews, by simply
> discarding those expectations and
> transforming Jesus into a completely new
> creature, one that seems almost wholly of
> his own making: *Christ.*"

While the small-c word *christ* is Greek for
messiah, Paul used the word in a new way,
with a capital C as if the title was a
surname, not unlike how the emperor
combined his name and title to be known
as Tiberius Caesar. In some ways, Paul's
Jesus Christ was not even human,
although he had the likeness of one. He
was a cosmic being, a "life-giving spirit"
who existed before time. He was the new
Adam, born not of dust but of heaven, and
would one day return to judge the world.
(1 Corinthians 15:42-49) While this
account is familiar to many Christians,
there was no precedent for it in Jewish
scripture, or in the words of Jesus as
recalled by the mother assembly in

Jerusalem – the people who actually walked with Jesus. Aslan describes this as "a firm indication that Paul's Christ was likely his own creation." Aslan points out that the all-powerful Jesus that appears in Paul's epistles does not even appear in the four gospels, which were written after Paul's epistles.

Finally, on his own, Paul claimed the authority to preach the gospel to the uncircumcised Gentiles. His second mission took him to Phrygia, Galatia, Macedonia, Philippi, Thessalonica, Berea, Athens, and Corinth. His third mission took him to Galatia, Phrygia, Corinth, Ephesus, Macedonia, and Greece, the whole time corresponding with the local congregations by letters, in Greek.

Needless to say, members of the mother assembly in Jerusalem, chief among them Jesus's brother James the Just, were not pleased. James would compare the Jews who were part of The Way, but had abandoned Mosaic Law, as those who "look at themselves in the mirror...and upon walking away, immediately forget what they looked like." (James 1:23-24)

Many contemporary accounts depict James the Just as a righteous man, living a life of poverty in Jerusalem and preaching the word of his brother Jesus, while at the same time insisting on strict adherence to Mosaic Law. His only deviation from Mosaic Law was the contention that Jesus was the messiah, something which the priests were willing to debate, to a point. Otherwise, "James was recognized by all for his unsurpassed piety and his tireless defense of the poor." The best indication of James' authority is when Peter, the "rock" of the gospels, who by then was then the bishop of Rome, addressed James the Just as the "bishop of bishops, who rules Jerusalem, the Holy Assembly of the Hebrews, and all the Assemblies everywhere."

Aslan describes how, around 50 C.E., "James and the apostles demanded that Paul come to Jerusalem to answer for his deviant teachings." James and Paul would soon become bitter rivals, but at the time James summoned him to Jerusalem, Paul had no choice but to submit to the head of the mother assembly.

Paul would describe the so-called Council of Jerusalem as an ambush by "false believers." (Galatians 2:1-10). Aslan cites to an incident where an "enemy," later identified as Paul, "attacks James in a fit of rage and throws him down the Temple stairs." Accusing him of antinomianism, James forced Paul to participate in a ritual purification (the Nazirite vow which included paying to shave his head) which humiliated Paul for appearing to renounce what he had preached.

As the members of The Way fought among themselves, Jerusalem itself was in open revolt against Roman authority. James and the apostles assumed that the end was near, and that Jesus's return was imminent. As it happens, the Romans arrested Paul in Jerusalem, probably thinking he was the enigmatic "Egyptian," a case of mistaken identity. Paul argued that he was a Roman citizen and, as such, was entitled to a trial. The authorities agreed, and sent him to Rome.

In 62 C.E., James the Just was arrested by the son of a high priest (a "great hoarder of money") who had assumed power in the void left after the Roman governor was assassinated. James was charged with blasphemy and stoned to death. The most devout and observant Jews in Jerusalem were outraged. Aslan points to this as evidence that James the Just was "the undisputed leader of the movement Jesus had left behind."

Although James' epistle did make it into the canonical books of the New Testament, Aslan asks the question, why is it that James has been "almost wholly excised from the New Testament and his role in the early church displaced by Peter and Paul in the imaginations of most Christians?" He assumes that the Book of James was probably based on the actual teachings of James the Just. Aslan concludes that James was probably excluded from the canon because he was Jesus's brother, which "became an obstacle to those who advocated the perpetual virginity of his mother Mary."

Focus on Peter and Paul also satisfied the need for an institutional central seat of power, which after James' death and the destruction of the Second Temple, shifted from Jerusalem to Rome. Aslan also recognizes that the Epistle of James is notable for "its passionate concern with the plight of the poor." In fact, "The Jerusalem assembly was founded by James upon the principle of service to the poor." (See James 5) Perhaps that message did not have universal appeal to the relatively wealthy Gentiles.

Meanwhile, back in Rome, Paul's attempts to preach were thwarted by Peter, now the first of the Twelve. As Aslan puts it, Rome was "in short, an anti-Pauline community." He goes on to recount how, in the year 64 C.E., the emperor Nero "seized Peter and Paul and executed them both for espousing what he assumed was the same faith...He was wrong." Peter was still struggling with appealing to Jews, while Paul's emphasis was by then completely on conversion of the Gentiles.

It is said that Paul was beheaded. Peter was probably crucified upside down, as he desired to suffer, considering himself unworthy to die the same way as his

Savior. Aslan does not address the possibility that Peter and Paul were blamed for the Great Fire of Rome which occurred on July 18, 64 C.E. Members of The Way who were convicted of conspiring to set the Fire of Rome, who for the first time were called Christians, "Mockery of every sort was added to their deaths. Covered with the skins of beasts, they were torn by dogs and perished, or were nailed to crosses, or were doomed to the flames and burnt, to serve as a nightly illumination, when daylight had expired."

It would be easy to see how some might conclude that the end of times was upon them.

The year 66 C.E. was also when the "Great Revolt" began, according to some, "in requital for" the martyrdom of James the Just. In Jerusalem, rebels and radicals such as the Zealots and Sicarii escalated their attacks on Romans, who responded by executing as many as 6,000 Jews, and sacking the Second Jewish Temple. At the Battle of Beth Horon, the Judeans responded by killing 6,000 Romans. Following that shocking defeat, the

Romans sent in general Vespasian, his son Titus, and sixty thousand soldiers, who over the course of several years, wore down the Judean resistance, breached Jerusalem's walls and, in Aslan's words: "unleashed an orgy of violence upon its residents. They butchered everyone in their path, heaping corpses on the Temple Mount. A river of blood flowed down the cobblestone streets."

The effect of the destruction of the Second Temple by the Romans in 70 C.E. cannot be understated. Everything that Second Temple Judaism ever stood for was gone. Tens of thousands were dead or enslaved, the rest were exiled, left to wander the land, searching to re-create their lives.

After the siege, with their sacred Temple in ashes, "[t]he Torah replaced the Temple in the center of Jewish life, and rabbinic Judaism emerged." Many Jews blamed the (capital Z) Zealots and the Sicarii for the loss of the Second Temple, and began to distance themselves from their messianic nationalistic fervor. Many Jews found themselves in Rome, including Peter's former interpreter, a scribe named John Mark, who "took up his quill and composed the first words to the first gospel written about the messiah known as Jesus of Nazareth."

It is important to note that the gospels and the epistles were not canonized into the New Testament until the Council of Nicea in 325 C.E. Between Jesus's death and the Council of Nicca, there were many contemporaneous writings which, depending on the region, were more "official" than others. Some of these writings were not selected for inclusion in the New Testament by the Council of Nicea, which was composed of Roman citizens. These "apocryphal" writings include the never-seen "Q," which is widely understood as the common source for the Gospels of Luke and Matthew. Aslan emphasizes, "Those who did know Jesus – those who followed him into Jerusalem...played a surprisingly small role in defining the movement Jesus left behind."

All of the canonical books of the New Testament were written in Greek, a language that most of Jesus's disciples in Jerusalem could not speak, let alone write. It's as if a French-speaking Canadian Muslim wrote the definitive biography of Richard Nixon in 2013. Aslan points out that of the epistles included in the New Testament, only seven were attributed to Jesus's actual disciples: James, Peter, and John. By contrast, fully fourteen epistles were either by or about the former Pharisee Paul who, as Aslan puts it, was "the deviant and outcast who was rejected and scorned by the leaders in Jerusalem."

The Gospel of Mark was chronologically the first canonical gospel, probably written in Rome a few years after Peter and Paul's death, between 68-73 C.E. The second was the Gospel of Matthew, probably written in Damascus (now part of the besieged Syria) between 70-100 C.E. The third was the Gospel of Luke which was probably written in the Greek city of Antioch (in modern day Turkey) between 80-100 C.E. The fourth was the Gospel of John, which was probably written in Ephesus (in present day Turkey) between 90-120 C.E.

Aslan emphasizes that each gospel had a different audience, and that the purpose of these gospels was to bring that audience into Christianity. After the destruction of the Second Temple, because Jesus's followers were "Scattered across the Roman Empire, it was only natural for the gospel writers to distance themselves from the Jewish independence movement by erasing, as much as possible, any hint of radicalism or violence, revolution or zealotry, from the story of Jesus, and to adapt Jesus's words and actions to the new political situation in which they found themselves." He says that the Jews "could either maintain their cultic connections...or they could divorce themselves from Judaism and transform their messiah from a fierce Jewish nationalist into a pacifist preacher of good works whose kingdom was not of this world."

So just as Ba'al was absorbed into the Roman cult of Saturn, what began as a Jewish movement known as The Way, was eventually absorbed into Roman culture and became Christianity. To the victors, they say, go the spoils. By 120 C.E., Aslan notes, "nearly half a century after the destruction of Jerusalem, Christianity was already a thoroughly Romanized religion, and Paul's Christ had long obliterated any last trace of the Jewish messiah in Jesus." Christianity would eventually become the official religion of Rome, and would survive the fall of the Roman Empire. Today Christianity is the world's biggest religion, with 2.2 billion adherents. Most Christians believe that Jesus was the Son of God, both fully divine and fully human, and was the savior of humanity prophesized in the Old Testament. As such, He is known as Jesus Christ. As a group, his followers are known not by his name, Yeshu or Jesus, but by his title – they are called Christians.

Aslan's *Zealot* obviously pokes some holes in commonly accepted Christian dogma about the historical Jesus. Many Christian conservatives have responded passionately. Glen Beck said: "[Aslan's] goal is to ... Change our history. Change our traditions." (Beck, 2013). Was Beck right? Can *Zealot* change Christian history and Christian tradition?

Chapter IV: Synopsis

Reza Aslan's point in *Zealot* is that there are two Jesuses: Jesus of Nazareth and Jesus the Christ. The former was a poor boy born in first century Galilee who became an influential preacher and who was crucified for sedition. The second is God incarnate who was born of a virgin, was crucified for our sins, and on the third day, rose from the dead in fulfillment of the scriptures. Which one is the real Jesus? The easy answer is that depends on whether you are a biblical historian or a person of faith. The harder answer is that both Jesuses are "real" and that the existence of one does not preclude the other.

Aslan summarized *Zealot's* thesis on NPR: "[The Apostles] were farmers and fisherman. These were illiterates; they could neither read nor write, so they couldn't really espouse Christology, high-minded theology about who Jesus was. They certainly couldn't write anything down. Instead, the task of spreading the Gospel message outside of Jerusalem, of really creating what we now know as

Christianity, fell to a group of urbanized, Hellenized, educated Jews in the Diaspora; [and] for [the Romans], having grown up immersed in this Hellenized, Romanized world, the concept of a God-man was something quite familiar. Caesar Augustus was a God-man. What we really see in these 20 years after Jesus's death is this process whereby this Jewish religion based on a Jewish revolutionary becomes transformed into a Roman religion, where Jesus is transformed from a Jewish conception of a Messiah to a kind of Roman demigod."

Initially, the book was met with righteous invective. Interviewer Lauren Green and evangelical preacher John S. Dickerson attacked the messenger for being Muslim: "[Aslan] is not an objective observer, but, to use his own word, a zealot, with religious motivation to destroy what Western culture has believed about its central figure for hundreds of years...

Zealot tries to demolish Christianity's most important doctrine about Jesus—that He claimed to be God.[2] *Zealot* concludes not with opinion or theory but with claimed fact that the faith of 2 billion Christians is historically impossible and irrational and therefore foolish." (Dickerson, 2013)

Glen Beck concluded that *Zealot* was part of a bigger conspiracy to destroy Christianity: "[Aslan's] goal is to cause doubt in the believers of Jesus and ultimately have them leave their faith like he did, so progressives will have more followers who can do whatever their hearts' desire tells them to do. Change our history. Change our traditions. That's what this is really all about." (Beck, 2013).

These critics are really frightened of the biblical message in *Zealot*. Is Aslan's goal to destroy what Western culture has believed about Jesus for hundreds of years? Is he seeking to entice Christians to

---

[2] As we will see in Chapter V, this is false. Jesus never claimed to be God.

leave their faith? Is he seeking to demolish Christianity's most important doctrines? Change Western history? Change traditions that have formed over millennia?

Not all reactions to *Zealot* have been negative. While interviewing Aslan on the friendly confines of The Daily Show, John Oliver said about the Jesus of Nazareth depicted in *Zealot*: "I liked this man. I liked this guy who was a day laborer who was probably illiterate, who was a radical nationalist. I liked this guy... He means more to me, you can have a personal relationship with this man. I just wonder how he would feel about 'Touchdown Jesus.'" (Oliver, 2013).

When it comes to *Zealot*, scholarly critics have been much more understated than the people at FoxNews, but no less critical. Interestingly, most of the scholarly (read: intelligent) critics seem to have been working off of the same talking points: 1) There's nothing new here, 2) the book is reductive fiction, 3) the book says more about the author than the subject, 4) the martyrs weren't fools, and 5) he's trying to launch a new cult.

What specifically are the critics saying about *Zealot*? Let's take a look.

Talking Point 1: Nothing New Here

Almost every essay criticizing *Zealot* begins with a line like this one by Kevin Hart: "Reza Aslan's *Zealot* is the latest in what might well be a never-ending series of 'lives of Jesus'... [it] tells scholars nothing new; it is a popularization of original research." (Hart, 2013). You can almost see Hart's eyes rolling as he writes. Softer, but still patronizing, Dale B. Martin ends his review with, "*Zealot* is not innovative or original scholarship, but it makes an entertaining read." (Martin, 2013).

What they are saying is that Jesus the man, Jesus of Nazareth, the historical Jesus, has already been studied for about 200 years, which is actually rather recent given that Jesus lived 2000 years ago. So how could there possibly be anything new in the field? Kevin Hart explores the three main phases in the quest for the historical Jesus. (Hart, 2013). The first "quest" started in the 18th century and ended in 1906 when Albert Schweitzer criticized these studies as little more than romance novels, never questioning the gospels, and allowing the authors to construct the portrait of Jesus that they wanted to see, creating their own idealized version of the historical Jesus.

The second quest introduced academic rigor into the study of the historical Jesus, but still usually relied on (and deferred to) the canonical texts of the bible, seeking mostly to harmonize them. The high water mark of the second quest is represented by the work of Raymond Brown, S.J., and John P. Meier's "magisterial" four-volume study, *A Marginal Jew: Rethinking the Historical Jesus* (1991-2009). (Meier, 1991-2009).

"Only with the third quest," says Hart, "which started in the 1980s, do we find Jesus viewed as Jewish, with a rich harvest of insight gained from meticulous historical criticism of Scripture, done by Jewish as well as Christian authors, from archeological evidence of life in the Holy Land under Roman occupation, and from the sharp lenses of modern historical investigation of the Mediterranean world." (Hart, 2013).

No doubt chief among the archeological evidence Hart refers to are the 1945 discovery of the Gnostic Gospels in Nag Hammadi in Egypt, and the 1946 discovery of the Dead Sea Scrolls at Khirbet Qumran in the West Bank. The translated Gnostic Gospels were not available until the 1970s, and the Dead Sea Scrolls were not available for study until 1991. Multi-disciplinary research into the historical Jesus, unhinged from but still emphasizing the canonical texts, did not begin in earnest until around that time. Critics fail to acknowledge that, in *Zealot*, Aslan conservatively eschews most of the apocryphal texts. Despite *Zealot's* success, John Dominic Crossan's ground-breaking *The Historical Jesus: The Life of a Mediterranean Jewish Peasant* (1993) (Crossan, 1993), which incorporates history, social anthropology, and literary analysis, still leads the genre in the third quest study of the historical Jesus.

So there actually is quite a lot of new material available in the study of the historical Jesus. A true multi-disciplinary approach has only been underway for twenty years. That's half the time that elapsed between the crucifixion and the Gospel of Mark.

Talking Point 2: Reductive Fiction

Most critics concur that *Zealot's* argument suffers because Aslan cherry-picks among biblical passages to make his point. As Allan Nadler puts it, "The only novelty in Aslan's book is his relentlessly reductionist, simplistic, one-sided and often harshly polemical portrayal of Jesus as a radical, zealously nationalistic, and purely political figure. Anything beyond this that is reported by his apostles is, according to Aslan, Christological mythology, not history." (Nadler, 2013). Andrei Codrescu compares Aslan to a novelist or film director, "The retelling disposes of all unnecessary material circulated against type." (Codrescu, 2013).

Nadler notes that Aslan "never provides his readers with so much as a hint of any method for separating fact from fiction in the Gospels." (Nadler, 2013). Recognizing academic disputes in the area, Nadler points out that Aslan creates a "Manichean dichotomy between the historical Jesus of Nazareth and mythical Jesus Christ of the Gospels, Aslan perceives everything as an either/or proposition—either the zealous, radical, and purely political Jesus of history, or the entirely fictional moral teacher and pacifistic Jesus of Christology." (Nadler, 2013). Dale B. Martin agrees, saying "Nowadays, most scholars believe that the Christian movement was much more diverse, even from its very beginnings." (Martin, 2013).

The critics are absolutely correct on the reductive point. Aslan fails to adequately establish a metric in his analysis to differentiate between historical and non-historical passages. Aslan's oft-repeated "all you need to know" line about the *titulus* on the cross actually highlights a weakness in his argument. How the Romans viewed Jesus has little to do with how the disciples, or for that matter Jesus himself, interpreted his ministry. Aslan should at least have given a nod to views opposing his central thesis. Coupled with Aslan's tireless self-promotion, which probably makes most academics cringe, the book's credibility suffers as a result. That said, *Zealot* was clearly written for the general reader. If anything, the ambiguity may spark the curious to conduct further scholarly reading about the historical Jesus. They need not refer to the notes at the end of *Zealot* though, the notes do not refer back to the body of the text, and are polemical when they should be irenic. They read more like spare parts tossed in at the end. As a practical matter, the notes are useless.

But to call the book fiction is simply insulting. *Zealot* is serious, well-researched historical non-fiction. To call it fiction because the author ignores contradictory passages in the bible is itself reductive. Remember, the cherry-picking argument cuts both ways. Because so many passages in the bible are vague and self-contradictory, anyone counter-arguing points in *Zealot* will likewise have to dismiss contradictory biblical passages to make their point. Abusive criticism is not helpful, it says more about the critic than it does about the author.

Talking Point 3: *Zealot* Says More About The Author Than The Subject

Most of Aslan's critics argue that *Zealot* says more about Aslan than it does about Jesus. This is simply a rip-off of Albert Schweitzer's criticism of the first quest studies in *The Quest of the Historical Jesus* (1906) (Schweitzer, 1906). Using this argument against a third quest study like *Zealot* smacks of intellectual laziness. According to this argument, first, anyone attempting to draw conclusions about the historical Jesus will necessarily make subjective judgments about what to include and what to exclude, and second, consciously or unconsciously, those judgments are agenda-driven. The second point is a meritless variant of Green and Dickerson's *ad hominem* argument – that a Muslim scholar can't make an objective conclusion about Jesus. The first point though, has merit. The historical record of Jesus's life is so thin and so contradictory, the amount of filling in required to paint a complete picture will necessarily include subjective judgments – judgments that academics sometimes make too quickly when trying to appeal to a broad audience. A study's worth should be judged only on the merits of those judgments.

Andrei Codrescu grabs this argument, saying: "On this subject, Reza Aslan is clear: 'Scholars tend to see the Jesus they want to see,' which is true enough. Unfortunately, he goes on to say, 'Too often they see *themselves* [italic in the original] — their own reflection — in the image of Jesus they constructed.' This is, I hope, untrue, because if Professor Aslan sees himself in the Jesus he's constructed we are in trouble." (Codrescu, 2013). (Talk about meta!) Ironically, by inserting his own subjective judgment into whether Aslan's subjective judgment means "trouble," Codrescu commits the very same error.

Talking Point 4: So Many Died It Must Be True

The fourth talking point is to condemn *Zealot* as insulting to the thousands of martyrs who died believing what Aslan refutes. Dr. Andre Villeneuve puts the point in equally historical terms and as an appeal *ad misericordiam*: "When we really try to think along those lines of what Aslan's trying to make us believe, it's really somewhat preposterous actually: that all these early martyrs and disciples were willing to die as martyrs for what, according to him, was a colossal lie, or myth." (Bunderson, 2013).

The appeal to pity should not fool anyone, but the historical portion of this argument, which according to *Zealot's* critics deals almost exclusively with the resurrection, has merit. In fact, Aslan makes that very point in Chapter 13 of *Zealot*, referring to the "nagging fact" that the people who supposedly witnessed

Jesus's resurrection endured gruesome deaths rather than recant their testimony that the resurrection actually happened. In a sense, this argument captures the essence of the discussion, and leads to the ultimate question of Jesus's divinity. Contrary to what the critics might imply, Aslan does not address the historicity of the resurrection in *Zealot*, saying that it is beyond the scope of historical analysis and is exclusively a matter of faith.

Talking Point 5: New Cult

Speaking of faith, the last standard "talking point" response to *Zealot* claims that Aslan is a leader in the brand new Cult of the Historical Jesus. The critics disagree as to the nature of this new cult, but to them it is a cult nonetheless. Kevin Hart calls it naturalism, the idea that only natural (as opposed to supernatural or spiritual) laws operate in the world. It is interesting how naming something marginalizes it in a way, as if to deny the supernatural is just another claim against the dogma of the Magisterium (the teaching authority of the Church). Using a double-negative, Dr. Andre Villeneuve calls it *anti-super*naturalism, "influenced by the Jesus seminar school," which in the 1980s and 1990s had proposed Jesus as nothing more than a rabbi, sage and healer. Charlotte Allen calls it "the latest installment in a vast body of literature reflecting the beliefs of a completely different religion: the Church of the Historical Jesus. ... The aim of this church, which has been around since the Enlightenment and its worship of rationalism, is to peel away the Gospel stories, with their virgin birth, their miracles and their walking on water, to uncover the 'real' Jesus, a demythologized, strictly human figure who didn't found Christianity and who stayed dead when he died." (Allen, 2013).

It would be easy to dismiss this "new cult" criticism as a variant of Dickerson's warning about the "destruction of Western culture," or Glen Beck's warning that *Zealot* is but one episode in the Progressive movement's campaign to "change our history, change our traditions." This indictment, though, if used to examine the nascent (capital H) Historical Jesus movement as a whole, could yield some interesting insights.

The Historical Jesus field is not a theological movement *per se*, but if enough Christians study Jesus of Nazareth, it could affect how they worship Jesus Christ. Would that necessarily be a *bad thing*? People like Dickerson and Beck, and for that matter Codrescu, Hart, Villeneuve, Nadler, Darrell Bock (Bock, 2013), and Charlotte Allen unanimously seem to think it would.

What would be the effect on Christianity if the historicity of events long preached as Christian dogma didn't actually happen? Does something have to be real to be true? Elie Wiesel said, "Some stories are true that never happened." The literature on the Historical Jesus has called into question the factual basis of just about every event in the gospel account of Jesus's life: the immaculate conception, the virgin birth, the perpetual virginity of Mary, Elizabeth's pregnancy with John the Baptist, appearances by angels, the birth in Bethlehem, the magi, the murder of the innocents, the flight to Egypt, the infant Jesus preaching in the Temple, Jesus's miracles, the trial before Caiaphas, the trial before Pontius Pilate, and yes, even the resurrection. What else is left?

Almost everyone, from St. Paul, to Aslan's critics, to Aslan himself, say that if you remove the resurrection from the timeline, you remove every basis for Christian worship. After all, Jesus would no longer be the Christian Christ, or for that matter the Jewish messiah. Put another way, if you remove every supernatural element from Jesus's timeline, most people agree that there would be no basis for the religious worship, because at that point he would only be Jesus of Nazareth.

Is that necessarily the case?

Chapter V: Thesis

Author Paulo Coelho said, "People see the world, not as it is, but as they are." This is known as confirmation bias, a variant of the law of the instrument: if all you have are hammers, every problem starts to look like a nail. Professor Peter Berger wrote about the Social Construction of Reality, which posited that what we perceive as "real" is a result of a highly specialized social structure, built not to see actual reality, but rather to see what will help us survive. Our perceptions and our cognitions are both biased and distorted. Authors David Foster Wallace and George Saunders were fascinated to the point of obsession by the notion that there is an unseen reality that is hidden in plain sight, which only becomes apparent in retrospect, if at all. Your eyes can always see the end of your nose, but your brain does not register it, because that would be distracting and therefore potentially fatal.

Lump all of these perception "defects" into the bucket called "cognitive biases," and you have a pretty good idea how people see, hear, and think. For instance, the creation narrative in Genesis recounts how God shaped the first man from dust and breathed life into him. God then created the first woman, from the man's rib. For most of us, the book of Genesis does not describe how humankind was actually created, we think of it as a metaphor. We see the dust and the rib, not as the actual stuff we were made of, but more as an allegory for the true nature of our creation, which still could be more "true" than the mutated strands of DNA that we "know" today are the scientific root of our physical existence.

But Genesis was not written for us, or by us. It was written sometime in the 5th century B.C.E., around the time of the destruction of the First Temple by the Babylonians. Over a hundred generations have lived since the Book of Genesis was written. That is twenty five centuries of human experience, human suffering, and human advances. Genesis was written to a completely different audience than us. People have changed, but the text has not. More than any building, the Book of Genesis is an obdurate memorial to the minds and souls of a people long since gone from this planet.

Five centuries after the Book of Genesis was written, the people of first century Judea were, by today's standards, poor and uneducated. They also experienced the world differently. Our experience of the world is much more defined by "fact" and "science." Almost everyone in the first century believed in magic, spirits, angels, visions, and voices coming down from the sky. If you believe in something, like the end of your nose, you will see it from time to time. What today might simply seem like natural occurrences, to people in the first century were signs full of symbolism and foreboding. God spoke to them in the wind. He speaks to us on cable television.

The people of Judea were deeply faithful. With the Roman occupation beginning in 63 B.C.E., their faith became fervor. For decades, rebel leaders sought to liberate the children of Israel from their Roman oppressors. Today they are either called "freedom fighters" or "terrorist leaders," depending on your perspective. To the Jews, they were called "messiah," saviors anointed by the king, and thus by God, to liberate the people from bondage.

The Romans were brutal, savagely putting down any uprising among the Judeans. Bodies were heaped upon bodies as their blood flooded the Second Temple. The people desperately wanted a savior from this horror. As earthly attempts failed, messianic sects formed, claiming that a messiah would come in judgment, as the end of the world was clearly at hand.

The Judean uprisings grew in pitch. In 66 C.E., 6,000 Roman soldiers were killed. In 70 C.E., the Romans responded by sacking the Second Temple and slaughtering thousands of Jews. In 132 C.E., Jewish rebels launched the Bar Kokhba revolt, a last attempt to reclaim their land. The Romans crushed the rebellion, killing 100,000 Jews while reducing the Second Temple, and all of Jerusalem with it, to rubble. Jerusalem was quite literally wiped off the map. The surviving Jews were sent into exile from the Holy Land, just as their ancestors had been sent to Babylon.

Jesus of Nazareth lived in Judea in the
midst of this troubled time. As outlined in
Chapter II, Jesus took up with a messianic
preacher, and after the preacher was
killed by the Romans, Jesus took over his
ministry, led his followers into Jerusalem,
and was himself killed by the Romans.
Over and over again, Aslan points to the
titulus on the cross as proof that Jesus
was crucified for sedition, saying that is all
we need to know about the life of Jesus.
No doubt it tells a lot, but Aslan's major
premise – that the purpose of Jesus's
ministry was to liberate the people from
Roman oppression, is over-simplified. To
learn what Jesus preached, read the
gospels.[3] Yes, perhaps Jesus meant that
the coin should be returned to Caesar, and
that the land was God's and should
rightfully be rendered unto Him, but

---

[3] Larry Hurtado concedes: "[I]t is now increasingly
accepted that the Gospels should be seen in the wider
context of Roman-era biographical-type writings, they
remain notable texts individually and collectively,
comprising a distinctive Christian sub-genre."

Jesus's ministry was about far more than the Roman occupation.

What do we know about Jesus's ministry? Look to the New Testament. But remember, the New Testament was written by and for people who quite literally believed in magic. Things in the bible that seem absurd today were common then. For instance, show your kids Episode 17 of *Father Knows Best*, where "Jim comes home after a bad day at work. Wanting to tell the family about his day, he is miffed when they ignore him. He starts complaining about everyone and everything around the house. Then he finds out Kathy broke a neighbor's window." Just half a century after that show aired, its reality is so far removed from our reality that it seems absurd. But that was reality for the Americans of 1956, and the jokes were actually funny. It is important to keep in mind that, when reading the bible, we are reading *Father Knows Best* forty times removed. It helps to keep in mind that we see a reality that first century Judeans could not see. It also helps to keep in mind that they saw a reality that today, *we* cannot see.

Scholars often refer to the "historicity" of a scriptural passage. "Historicity" is a fancy word for whether or not something actually happened (not necessarily if it is *true*). So if you doubt the historicity of God's forming the first man out of dust, as opposed to some variant of evolution, then you may be what some may call a bible skeptic.

Aslan's book is written to appeal to bible skeptics, because it points out the problems with the historicity of many of the New Testament's supposedly factual descriptions of the life of Jesus. Knowing what we know today about biology, does the immaculate conception make any sense? Does the virgin birth make sense? If you are being honest with yourself, the answer is no. (That would be doubly so if you are a mother.) Knowing what we know today about the history of the Roman occupation of Judea, does it make any sense that there was a census which forced Joseph and Mary, who were not Roman citizens, to travel somewhere they did not live, just to be counted? Religious scholars seem to agree that there's no way

Jesus was born in Bethlehem while Joseph was being counted.

So, if we concede that man was not formed by dust, that concession casts everything else in the bible in doubt too, right? Some stories in the bible are metaphors, some are literal fact, but which ones are which? That is the grey area, and with respect to the study of the historical Jesus, the grey area is vast.

Over the centuries, the historicity of a seemingly simple fact like the virgin birth has taken on huge significance because it ultimately leads to the *big fact*: resurrection. A central tenet of Christianity is that, after the crucifixion, Jesus rose from the dead in fulfillment of the scriptures. Knowing what we do today about decomposition of a corpse, we know that after three days, rigor mortis has set in and has dissipated, the skin has become discolored, the body has begun to bloat and putrefy. These effects are irreversible. Could such a body become re-animated? The honest answer is no. And it is okay to think that, you have a post-Enlightenment rational mind. That is how you're supposed to think. You know that if a supernatural force somehow brought a three day old corpse back to life, it would be more zombie than savior. The historicity of the big fact raises a big question, as put by Aslan: "Without the resurrection, the whole edifice of Jesus's claim to the mantle of the messiah comes crashing down."

Does it?

First, claiming "the mantle of the messiah" is different than claiming divinity. The one who is divine in the theological sense is God. Call it Elohim, call it YHVH, Jesus never claimed that he was God. I'll say that again – Jesus never said that he was God. That was left for his followers to say. As Aslan put it in an interview:

> Q: "Would you lean toward Nietzsche who said the last Christian died on the cross?"

> A: "I would change it around, I would not call Jesus a Christian [at all]... Prophets are not inventors of religion. Jesus did not invent Christianity. Moses did not invent Judaism. Siddhartha Gautama did not

invent Buddhism. Mohammed did not invent Islam. Prophets are reformers, their task is to take the religious and social and political milieu in which they live and to reform it, to recast it, to renew it in a sense. It's often the case that it's left to the followers of the prophet, after the prophet has died, to then take this herculean task of taking the words and taking the actions of the prophet that they knew and formulating it into an institution, creating a religion out of it. Which is frankly why we often are...are met with this uncomfortable reality that there is often so much of a difference between the values that are preached by the prophet and those that are espoused by the institutions that arose from the teachings of the prophet."

Who was Jesus? That is the ten dollar question – he asked it himself ("Who do you say I am?" Mark 8:29). As most people see it, the question is whether Jesus was divine. Some might go further, and ask what "divine" means.

The New Testament has many "High Christologies" – assertions of Jesus's divinity, which have been analyzed for thousands of years by thousands of brilliant scholars, who to this day have not come to a consensus on the answer. In the New Testament, the scholars' main source material, Jesus is called the Messiah, the lamb of God, the Son of Man, the Son of God, and the King of the Jews. Partly because the bible is so internally contradictory, no one seems to have a clear idea about what these titles mean, whether they are properly applied to Jesus, or if Jesus intended them to be applied to him. Was Jesus the Messiah? The Son of Man? The Son of God? Was Jesus the King of the Jews? All of the above? None of the above? The honest inquirer will search the bible and its commentary in vain for a clear answer to that question.

Likewise, there is the question of Jesus's mission, known in scholarly circles as his eschatology. As written in the New Testament, when discussing his mission, Jesus often refers to the Kingdom of God. Aslan posits that the Kingdom of God is where God becomes the sole sovereign, not just over Israel, but over the whole world. He characterizes the Beatitudes as what the poor can expect in the future Kingdom of God, which will come after "the destruction of the present order." Aslan mocks the loving-your-enemies and turning-the-other-cheek Jesus as "a complete fabrication."

But what is the Kingdom of God? The scholars, the gospel writers, and Jesus himself couldn't seem to figure that out either: there is the earthly Kingdom of God which supposedly is coming, and there is the heavenly Kingdom of God which we aspire to enter. Are they the same? Aslan acknowledges that "It is difficult to know whether [even Jesus] had a unified conception of it."

Ultimately, as Aslan puts it, Jesus's mission and his divinity are matters of faith. The question of his divinity is particularly difficult to reconcile with reality as we see it today.

Three of the four gospels tell the story of Peter's declaration. When Jesus asked the disciples "Who do you say I am?" Peter answered, "You are the Messiah." Aslan points out that Jesus did not accept or reject the title, but responded by sternly ordering the disciples not to tell anyone. This is known as the "messianic secret." (Mark 8, Matthew 16, Luke 9). It's sort of like if a big brother asks his little brother who broke their dad's bowling trophy. The little brother says, "You broke it," and the big brother responds, "You're very clever, but don't tell anyone." The big brother has some plausible deniability there – he never really came out and said, "You're right, I did it," but he doesn't deny it either.

Aslan points to the Gospel of Mark, where Caiaphas asks Jesus directly, "Are you the messiah?" Jesus answers succinctly, "I am,"[4] but then goes on to muddy his answer with "an ecstatic exhortation, borrowed directly from the book of Daniel." Mark 14:61-62. Aslan submits

---

[4] In Matthew 26:64 and Luke 22:70 Jesus responds to Caiaphas's question with some variant of "you have said" or "you say I am." John 18:19-24 omits Caiaphas's question altogether.

that "The first century Jews who wrote about Jesus had already made up their minds about who he was. They were constructing a theological argument about the nature and function of Jesus *as Christ*, not composing a historical biography about a human being." (Emphasis in the original.)

This is supported by the transfiguration, the supernatural follow-up to Peter's declaration. In the transfiguration, the Apostles Peter, James, and John accompanied Jesus to a mountain, where Jesus was transfigured in "dazzling white," and a voice said, "This is my Son, the Beloved, listen to him!" (Mark 9, Matthew 17, Luke 9). Without saying as much, Aslan challenges the historicity of this story, pointing out that the "parallels between the so-called transfiguration story and the Exodus account of Moses receiving the law on Mount Sinai are hard to miss." He adds that that the title "the Beloved" supposedly used by God to describe Jesus, is also what God called King David.

So did Jesus himself ever declare that he was the Messiah, or as it is translated in Greek, the Christ? Aslan concludes that he did not: "there exists not a single definitive messianic statement from Jesus himself, not even at the very end when he stands before the high priest Caiaphas and somewhat passively accepts the title that others keep foisting upon him."

A noteworthy fact is that the (lower-case-m) messiah had no divine nature in the Jewish tradition, he was a man "anointed" with divine authority to save the Jews from bondage. Elijah was a prophet, not a god, he had no divine nature. Moses was a liberator, not a god, he had no divine nature. David was a king, not a god, he had no divine nature. Yet they were all called messiah. Aslan points out that Jesus did not liberate the Jews from the Romans, which is what Jesus's contemporaries probably assumed would be the messiah's mission. Aslan's explanation of the messianic secret, that Jesus really did think that he was the messiah, but spoke in code to avoid being arrested for sedition, characterizes Jesus as a rather timid and cowardly figure, and ignores the fact that if that was Jesus's strategy, it failed. One reviewer called that view "silly." (Carey, 2013).

There are several filial terms used in the New Testament to describe Jesus, such as the "Son of Man," the "Son of the Blessed," and the "Son of God." The Son of God was prophesized in Psalm 2:7 ("You are my son, today I have begotten you. Ask of me, and I will surely give the nations as your inheritance, and the very ends of the earth as your possession. You shall break them with a rod of iron, you shall shatter them like earthenware.") Was this Son of God a divine being? True to his thesis, Aslan says that, "Contrary to Christian conceptions, the title 'Son of God' was not a description of Jesus's filial connection to God but rather the traditional designation for Israel's kings."

The concept of a capital-M Messiah, a divine Son of God, a man who is one in being with the Father, was never part of the Jewish tradition. In the Gospel of

John, Jesus is the *Logos*, the "pre-incarnate" Son of God, and the word became flesh when Jesus was born.[5] Closely related is the idea of consubstantiality, the notion that Jesus was one in substance with God, one in being with the Father, which is a uniquely Greco-Roman idea. Human demi-gods were common in Greco-Roman culture. The Latin word *constubstantialis* comes from the Greek word ομοούσιος or *homoousian*. There is no equivalent word in Hebrew. The proposition that Jesus had a divine nature arose while Paul was actively trying to convert these Greco-Roman gentiles. Aslan asserts that this was not a coincidence.

Just as with the messianic secret, Jesus also rebuffed those who called him the "Son of God," referring to himself (*81 times*) as the very human "Son of Man."

---

5 Hurtado and Boyarin discuss the Logos at some length. In short, the Logos is a creature of Greek philosophy of reasoned discourse. Its sister is Sophia which means "wisdom." Philo of Alexandria was the main proponent of Jesus as the Logos, and his influence is very apparent in the Gospel of John.

Larry Hurtado points out that in Hebrew (*ben 'adam*) and Aramaic (*bar 'enosh*), the lower-case "[a] son of man" is simply a way of referring to a human being. (Hurtado, 2010). According to Aslan, the consensus view is that (capital-S, capital-M) titular use of the term "Son of Man" refers to an unnamed king mentioned in an apocalyptic vision in the Book of Daniel. Hurtado points out that the term is used as a title only on Jesus's lips. (Hurtado, 2010). Aslan adds that no one – from the first century Jews to today's scholars, really knows what that title means. Aslan nonetheless concludes that, by referring to himself as the Son of Man, Jesus saw himself as a Davidic king, destined to "restore the nation of Israel to its former glory." In other words, if Jesus was a Davidic King he would be, like David, human.

Daniel Boyarin concludes the exact opposite. In his book *The Jewish Gospels: the Story of the Jewish Christ* (New Press 2012) (Boyarin, The Jewish Gospels, 2012), Boyarin argues that under Jewish scripture, the term Son of Man indicates the *divine*, while the Son of God is a *human* who inherits David's throne. Boyarin's posits that the Second Temple Jews were binitarian, meaning they recognized that there could be two divine powers. While Aslan maintains that the notion of a divine messiah was foreign to first century Jews, Boyarin says that is not the case at all. Reviewing Boyarin's book, Peter Schäfer points out: "the evolving Christology of the New Testament and the early Church—that is, the idea of Jesus being essentially divine and human, the divine-human Messiah and Son of his Father in heaven—is deeply engrained in the Jewish tradition that preceded the New Testament." (Schafer, 2012).

We can take from this discussion that, regardless of whether there was a precedent for Jesus's divinity, for the Christology of the new church, the answer to the question of whether or not Jesus had a divine nature, was "evolving."

Did Jesus see himself as divine? This is impossible to know, because Jesus did not write the gospels. We will never know if

George Zimmerman stopped Trayvon Martin because of racial bias, and we will never know if Jesus considered himself to be God (or *a* god). Who knows? Perhaps Jesus loudly proclaimed his divinity in life, and the gospel writers removed these references in order to avoid blasphemy charges. We don't know. All we do know is, even if Jesus *thought* he was God, at least according to the New Testament, he never said as much.

So if the answer is in the texts, then there are millions of possible answers to the question of Jesus's divinity. Each passage has its own meaning, how conflicting passages are resolved affects that meaning. For example, Michael Heiser starts with Psalm 82:1-6, which refers to the "divine council." In the psalm, God (*elohim*, in the singular) chastises the divine council of <u>gods</u> (*elohim*, in the plural), for showing partiality to the wicked and not giving justice to the weak and the orphan.

According to Heiser, this passage is significant because Jesus refers to it when the Jews ask him: "How long will you keep us in suspense? If you are the Messiah, tell us plainly." Of course, Jesus does not tell them plainly. Instead, he makes an oblique reference to sheep, concluding with "The Father and I are one," whatever that means. They prepare to stone him for blasphemy. He asks them why, and they respond:

> "because you, though only a human being, are making yourself God (*theon*, in the singular)."

> Jesus answered, "Is it not written in your law, '<u>I said, you are gods</u>'? (*theoi*, in the plural, the referenced to Psalm 82) If those to whom the word of God came were called 'gods' – and the scripture cannot be annulled – can you say that the one whom the father has sanctified and sent into the world is blaspheming because I said, 'I am God's Son'? If I am not doing the works of my Father, then do not believe me. But if I do them, even though you do not believe me, believe the works, so that you may know and understand that the Father is in me and I am in the Father." John 10:34-38 (emphasis added).

This passage is frequently cited as "High Christology" because Jesus declared that he was the (capital-S) Son of God. Notice: 1) The gospel writer, not Jesus, chose to capitalize the S, 2) Jesus did not declare himself to be *God*, as the Jews accused, he declared that he was God's s*on*, and 3) Jesus interpreted the Psalm to mean those to whom the word of God came were "called gods." Was word of God Philo's *Logos*, or was it the word that Jesus himself taught?

There is only one God. Christianity is a monotheistic religion. It follows that God's Son (or anyone to whom God's word came) cannot have a divine nature in a monotheistic religion, right? The answer shows the evolving Christology that Schäfer referred. Heiser starts by asking if there is only one God, then how can there be a divine council comprised of many gods? The psalm suggests that early Israelites may have been polytheistic. Some scholars suggest that their polytheism had evolved into either monotheism or "binitarian monotheism" by the time of Second Temple Judaism. Heiser points out that "Since the Hebrew Bible is clear that there are other sons of God ... New Testament writers clarify that

Jesus, as the same essence as the Father, is unique among all heavenly sons of God."[6] (Heiser, 2011).

Larry Hurtado sees "a 'binitarian' devotional pattern [in the New Testament], in which Jesus is uniquely linked with God, not as a second or subordinate deity, and not at all at the expense of God in belief and devotion, but as the one who reflects and shares in God's glory." Hurtado concludes that early Christian binitarianism eventually evolved into post-Nicean monotheism. So, in sum, there were many gods, then there was one God, then God had a Son, and now they are one in substance and being, where Jesus is "the image of the invisible God,

---

[6] Jesus's divinity represents the fault line on which Christianity splits from Judaism. The last gospel, the Gospel of John, says, "And the Word became flesh and lived among us, and we have seen his glory, the glory as of the Father's only son, full of grace and truth." John 1:14. When the word became flesh, Christians adopted a Hellenist *Logos* theology, and parted ways with their Jewish brethren. As Boyarin puts it, "Rabbinic Judaism...can be seen as a nativist reaction movement that imagines itself a community free of Hellenism." (Boyarin, The Gospel of the Memra: Jewish Binitarianism and the Prologue to John, 2001).

the firstborn of all creation," and is indwelt by "all the fullness of God." (Hurtado, 2010).

All very heady stuff, but is this what Jesus meant when responding to the Jew's accusation that he called himself God? In the Book of John, Jesus said that in Psalm 82 "those to whom the word of God came were called 'gods.'" But that is not what Psalm 82 says. It doesn't identify those who were called "gods" at all, it simply identifies them as lower gods. In Psalm 82, God exhorts these lower gods to "Give justice to the weak and the orphan; maintain the right of the lowly and the destitute. Rescue the weak and the needy; deliver them from the hand of the wicked."

Is this the reality hiding in plain sight? Is Jesus saying here that all of us have a divine nature? Was Jesus saying that we invoke our own divine nature when we tend to the poor and the weak? That certainly would be consistent with his ministry. The prayer he gave us begins "Our Father," not "*my* Father." Start

where the gospels begin: Ἐ ν ἀ ρ χ ῇ ἦ ν ὁ
λ ό γ ο ς , "in the beginning was the
word." Here are Jesus's actual words, as
recounted in the gospels:

> "The spirit of the Lord is upon me,
> because he appointed me to preach the
> gospel to the poor. He has sent me to
> proclaim release to the captives, and
> recovery of sight to the blind, to set free
> those who are downtrodden, to proclaim
> the favorable year of the Lord." Luke 4:18-
> 19.

> "Blessed are you who are poor, for yours is
> the kingdom of God. Blessed are you who
> hunger now, for you shall be satisfied.
> Blessed are you who weep now, for you
> shall laugh." Luke 6:20-21.

> "But woe to you who are rich, for you are
> receiving your comfort in full... Woe to
> you who are well-fed now, for you shall be
> hungry." Luke 6:24-25.

> "Beware, and be on your guard against
> every form of greed; for not even when
> one has an abundance does his life consist
> of his possessions." Luke 12:15.

"One thing you still lack; sell all that you possess and distribute it to the poor, and you shall have treasure in heaven; and come, follow me." Luke 18:22.

"How hard it will be for those who are wealthy to enter the kingdom of God!" Mark 10:23.

"Again I say to you, it is easier for a camel to go through the eye of a needle, than for a rich man to enter the kingdom of God." Matthew 19:23.

"No one can serve two masters; for either he will hate the one and love the other, or he will be devoted to one and despise the other. You cannot serve God and wealth." Matthew 6:24.

"Truly I say to you, to the extent that you did not do it to one of the least of these, you did not do it to me." Matthew 25:45.

One consistent theme in Jesus's ministry is that his divine nature, our divine nature, is based on service to the poor. It is based on words and deeds. In Jesus's own words, Gods are "those to whom the word of God came...[B]elieve the works, so that you may know and understand that the Father is in me and I am in the Father." Perhaps Jesus is saying here that the mission of service to the poor is what makes us divine.

Does that lesson depend on Jesus's resurrection from the dead for its truth? Absolutely not.

Does Jesus have to be God to be worthy of our faith? Muslims fervently believe that the prophet Mohammed was *not* divine. Islam teaches that Mohammed died and was buried, yet his earthly message lives on. Perhaps Jesus's words can likewise survive the death of his earthly body. Perhaps what Jesus said is still true, even if he wasn't God incarnate. Hurtado warns that popular Christian piety often has Jesus effectively displacing God. After all, Christianity is not about the worship of Jesus, it is about the worship of God. As Aslan put it on the Daily Show: "You can be a follower of Jesus and not be a Christian, just as you can be a Christian and not be a follower of Jesus, if you know what I mean." (Oliver, 2013). Perhaps we could see Jesus of Nazareth as a human prophet and still be fully Christian.

Perhaps all this discussion about divinity, this debate about the historicity of the supernatural, is distracting us from the actual message of Jesus's ministry.

Like Jesus said: sell your possessions, give the money to the poor, and follow Him. Stephen and the rich ruler from first century Judea did just that. Perhaps Jesus is saying to us today: "Go and do likewise."

Bibliography

Allen, C. (2013, August 4). Reza Aslan's 'new' take on Jesus. Retrieved from L.A. Times: http://articles.latimes.com/2013/aug/04/opinion/la-oe-allen-reza-aslan-and-jesus-20130804

Aslan, R. (2013). Zealot: The Life and Times of Jesus of Nazareth. New York: Random House.

Beck, G. (2013, July 31). Who is Reza Aslan? Glenn exposes his progressive record. Retrieved from www.glennbeck.com: http://www.glennbeck.com/2013/07/31/who-is-reza-aslan-glenn-exposes-his-progressive-record/

Bock, D. (2013, August 12). When Scholarly Skepticism Encounters Jesus Christ. Retrieved from The Gospel Coalition: http://thegospelcoalition.org/blogs/tgc/2013/08/12/when-scholarly-skepticism-encounters-jesus-christ/

Boyarin, D. (2001). The Gospel of the Memra: Jewish Binitarianism and the Prologue to John. Retrieved from Michael S Heiser: http://michaelsheiser.com/TwoPowersInHeaven/Boyarin%20Memra.pdf

Boyarin, D. (2012). The Jewish Gospels. New York: New Press.

Bunderson, C. (2013, August 10). Controversial book's claims about Jesus are 'nothing new'. Retrieved from Catholic News Agency: http://www.catholicnewsagency.com/news/controversial-books-claims-about-jesus-are-nothing-new/

Carey, G. (2013, July 30). Reza Aslan on Jesus: A Biblical Scholar Responds. Huffington Post Religion. Retrieved from http://www.huffingtonpost.com/greg-carey/the-social-shape-of-divin_b_3707804.html

Codrescu, A. (2013, August 11). Marx, Che, Jesus. Retrieved from L.A. Review of Books: http://lareviewofbooks.org/review/marx-che-jesus

Crossan, J. D. (1993). The Historical Jesus: The Life of a Mediterranean Jewish Peasant. New York: HarperOne.

Dickerson, J. S. (2013, July 24). Liberal media love new Jesus book 'Zealot', fail to mention author is Muslim. Retrieved from FoxNews.com: http://www.foxnews.com/opinion/2013/07/22/liberal-media-love-new-jesus-book-zealot-fail-to-mention-author-is-muslim/

Gainor, D. (2013, August 1). Liberal media sharks continue feeding frenzy over 'Zealot' interview. Retrieved from FoxNews.com: http://www.foxnews.com/opinion/2013/08/01/lefty-media-sharks-continue-feeding-frenzy-over-zealot-interview/

Green, L. (2013, July 26). 'Zealot' author Reza Aslan responds to critics. Retrieved from FoxNews.com: http://video.foxnews.com/v/2568059649001

Hallowell, B. (2013, July 29). The 5 Most Awkward Moments During Journalist's Contentious Interview With Muslim Author Behind Jesus Book. Retrieved from The Blaze: http://www.theblaze.com/stories/2013/07/29/the-5-most-awkward-moments-during-journalists-contentious-interview-with-muslim-author-behind-jesus-book/

Hart, K. (2013, August 11). A Never-Ending Quest. Retrieved from L.A. Review of Books: https://lareviewofbooks.org/review/78659/

Heiser, M. S. (2011). Jesus' Quotation of Psalm 82:6 in John 10:34: A Different View of John's Theological Strategy. Retrieved from The Divine Council: http://www.thedivinecouncil.com/Psa82John10.pdf

Hurtado, L. (2010, July). Christology. Retrieved from Larry Hurtado blog: http://larryhurtado.files.wordpress.com/2010/07/chris tology-nidb.pdf

Martin, D. B. (2013, August 5). Sill a Firebrand, 2,000 Years Later. Retrieved from New York Times: http://www.nytimes.com/2013/08/06/books/reza-aslans-zealot-the-life-and-times-of-jesus-of-nazareth.html?pagewanted=all&_r=0

Meier, J. P. (1991-2009). A Marginal Jew: Rethinking the Historical Jesus. New York: Anchor Bible.

Nadler, A. (2013, August 11). What Jesus Wasn't: Zealot. Retrieved from Mosaic Magazine: http://mosaicmagazine.com/picks/2013/08/jesus-was-no-zealot/?utm_source=Mosaic+Daily+Email&utm_campa ign=c339ac9a05-Mosaic_2013_8_13&utm_medium=email&utm_term=0_0b0517b2ab-c339ac9a05-41171769

Oliver, J. (2013, July 17). Exclusive - Reza Aslan Extended Interview Pt.3. Retrieved from The Daily Show: http://www.thedailyshow.com/watch/wed-july-17-2013/exclusive---reza-aslan-extended-interview-pt--3

Schafer, P. (2012, May 18). The Jew Who Would Be God. Retrieved from New Republic: http://www.newrepublic.com/article/103373/books-and-arts/magazine/jewish-gospels-christ-boyarin

Schiffman, L. H. (n.d.). Palestine Under Roman Rule: Judea becomes a Roman tributary. Retrieved August 14, 2013, from My Jewish Learning: http://www.myjewishlearning.com/history/Ancient_an d_Medieval_History/539_BCE-632_CE/Palestine_Under_Roman_Rule.shtml

Schweitzer, A. (1906). The Quest of the Historical Jesus. London: A&C Black, Ltd.

Wilson, A. (2003). Romanizing Baal: The Art of Saturn Worship In North Africa. Retrieved from University of Oxford: http://users.ox.ac.uk/~corp0057/Romanizing%20Baal.pdf

Made in the USA
Columbia, SC
17 November 2023

26659748R00067